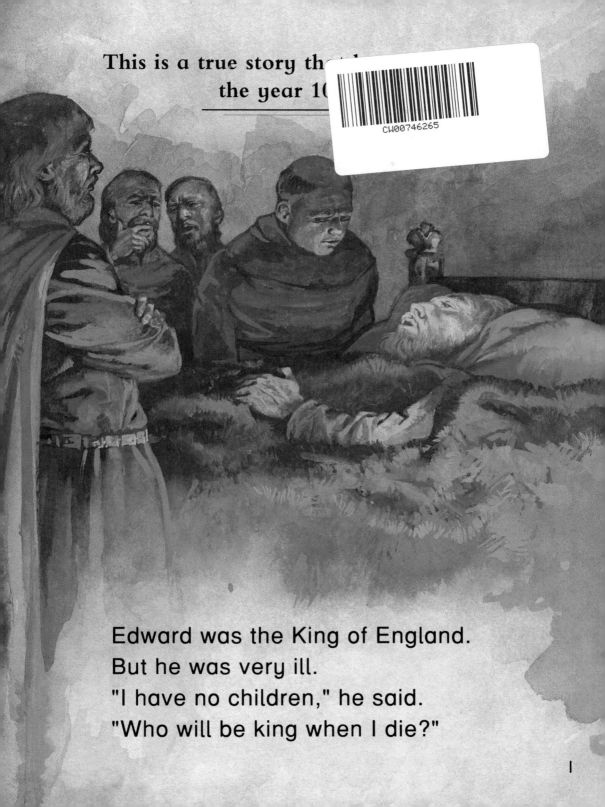

This is a true story th~~at~~ the year 10

Edward was the King of England.
But he was very ill.
"I have no children," he said.
"Who will be king when I die?"

King Edward called for Harold.
Harold was one of the most important
people in England.
"You must become the
next king," said Edward.

Edward died and Harold was made
King of England.

Across the sea in Normandy lived
a great lord called William.
William was very angry to hear the news.
"Edward and Harold promised me I would
be the next king!" he said.

William said, "We will sail across the sea
and fight Harold!"
His men cut down trees to build ships.

5

William and his men carried their
armour onto the ships.
They took spears and swords and
lots of arrows.
Even their horses went on the ships.

The ships sailed across the sea to England.
They landed at a place near Hastings.
But Harold was not there.

A Viking king had also sailed to
England to fight Harold.
Harold and his men defeated the Vikings.
"Now we must march to
fight William," said Harold.

Harold's men marched a long way to meet William.
They were very tired when they arrived at Hastings.

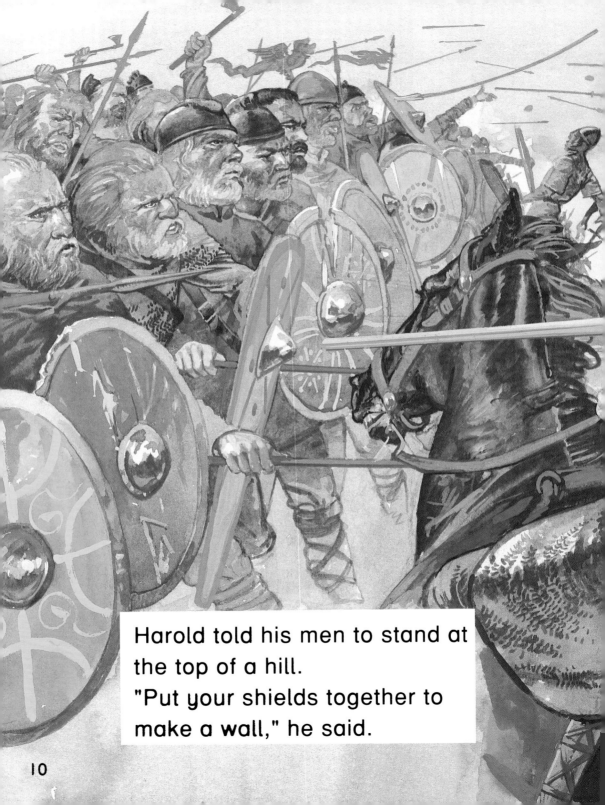

Harold told his men to stand at the top of a hill.
"Put your shields together to make a wall," he said.

William and his men came up the hill.
But the wall of shields pushed them back.

William fell off his horse.
"Are you hurt?" cried his men.

William got back on his horse.
He took off his helmet to
show his men he was not hurt.

Then William said, "Shoot your
arrows high into the sky."
The arrows went high into the sky and
over the wall of shields.

The arrows killed many of Harold's men.
William's men broke down the
shield wall and killed Harold.

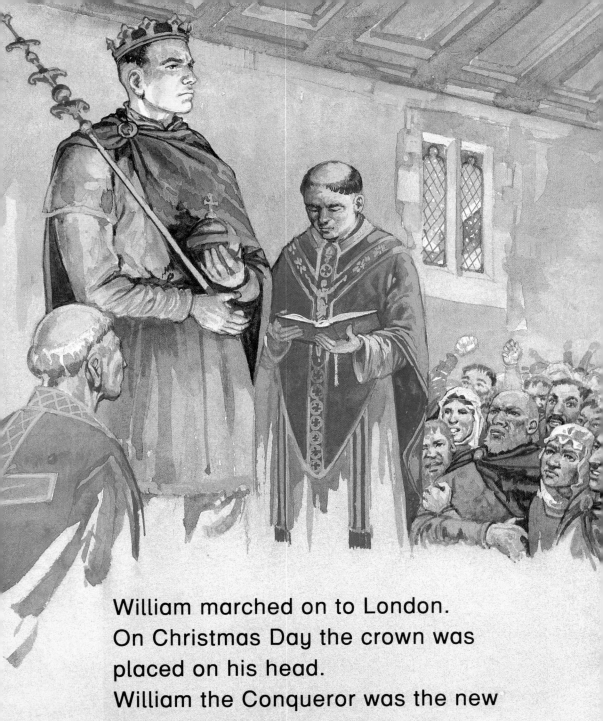

William marched on to London.
On Christmas Day the crown was
placed on his head.
William the Conqueror was the new
King of England.